MW01256763

Shaking the Family Tree

A Journey from Addiction to Recovery

Dallas H

PUBLISHING

Green Bay, WI 54311

Shaking the Family Tree: A Journey from Addiction to Recovery by Dallas H, copyright © 2017 by Dallas H.

This book is a true story about the real life of Dallas H. Permission has been obtained where possible for the use of names in the book, and changed, where persons wanted their identity to remain anonymous.This book reflects the opinions of the author and her life's decisions. Written Dreams Publishing does not approve, condone or disapprove of these opinions. It is up to the reader to make their own decisions.
    All rights reserved. In accordance with the U.S. Copyright Act of 1976, no part of this publication may be reproduced, distributed, or transmitted in any form or by any means, or stored in a database or retrieval system, without prior written permission of the publisher, Written Dreams Publishing, Green Bay, WI 54311.

A special thank you to the following individuals and organizations for their assistance: Alcoholics Anonymous World Services, ACA World Service Organization, Claudia Black, Ph.D., and her book, *It Will Never Happen to Me*, and Sharon Wegscheider-Cruse and Joseph Cruse, and their book, *Understanding Co-Depenency (the Science Behind It and How Break the Cycle).*

The Twelve Steps are reprinted with permission of Alcoholics Anonymous World Services, Inc. ("A.A.W.S.") Permission to reprint the Twelve Steps does not mean that A.A.W.S. has reviewed or approved the contents of this publication, or that A.A. necessarily agrees with the views expressed herein. A.A. is a program of recovery from alcoholism only- use of the Twelve Steps in connection with programs and activities which are patterned after A.A., but which address other problems, or in any other non-A.A., does not imply otherwise.

In accordance with its traditions, ACA World Service Organization expressly disclaims any association with any authors or books, or with any retailers and their affiliates.

This book is licensed for your personal enjoyment. This book may not be re-sold or given away to other people. If you would like to share this book with another person, please purchase an additional copy for each recipient. If you're reading this book and did not purchase it, or it was not purchased for your use only, then please purchase your own copy. Thank you for respecting the hard work of this author.

Editing: Brittiany Koren
Cover art design and Layout: Ed Vincent of ENC Graphics.
Cover Images: Shutterstock.com
Category: Self-Help/Inspirational Prose & Poetry
Description: A woman's struggle with alcoholism addiction and her journey to recovery.
Paperback ISBN: 978-0-9987623-8-8
Ebook ISBN: 978-0-9987623-9-5
Library of Congress Catalog Info: Applied For.
First Edition published by Written Dreams Publishing April, 2017

Green Bay, WI 54311

This book is dedicated to anyone out there who thinks that they may be suffering from alcohol or drug addiction. Be it huffed, puffed, snorted, injected, popped or ingested. It is a thief that will take away all of your hopes, your dreams, and perhaps, even your life. Your friends, family, and all of your relationships will suffer, often in silence, as they ride that elevator down with you, to your bottom.

Our stories may not be exactly alike. Our drinking and using patterns may vary. But the most damaging thread that weaves all of our fabric into a shared tapestry is a three-syllable word: *Denial*. It is the blindfold that we wear to our own execution.

Alcoholic

I've trudged many miles to get to this; my vanishing point. I have not traveled alone. I drag behind me generations of my kind. We often travel in packs, keeping others at bay, hoarding our secret. The vast terrain that has claimed many of us is strewn with the souls of those who sought escape from poverty, abuse, low self-esteem, and life in general. We found a magic elixir. It became our family's coat of arms.

> seduction
> hides inside a Goddess
> venus flytrap

For a while, it erased our fears and insecurities. We gulped greedily from its promise as it seeped through the cracks in our armor. We dressed in layers of false courage, fluffed our feathers and strutted across life's stage, immune to the snickers of a disgusted audience. We cast aside our problems and they became the property of those we loved. Then, without warning, It betrayed us.

> heir declines offer
> cannot afford to pay
> inheritance tax

How does one measure loss? In increments of currency, in a log of failures penned in stained tears, or perhaps, on the pages of our calendars crammed full of wasted years? I used to think that once important things were declared lost, they were gone forever. But, I am living proof that sometimes those things we hold most dear can be retrieved in even better condition than they were when we so carelessly misplaced them.

****

Three months had passed since our last visit to Chit-Chat, but I couldn't let go of the reflection of sorrow captured in the rearview mirror that day. It continued to haunt me. I tried to focus on the scenery, but the image of Luke, tears streaming down his cheeks, hands shaking so hard he could hardly steady the bottle of warm beer, it trickling down his chin, was embedded in the furthest reaches of my soul. I was that person with a toothache who subconsciously trains his tongue to go where the pain is. I spent the entire trip pushing the replay button.

Chit-Chat, our destination was the original site of Caron's substance abuse and treatment facility. It was a scorching Sunday afternoon in August 1987. Wrapped in fear, trepidation, and a smidgeon of curiosity, I lugged my suitcase out of my sister Gerri's trunk and reluctantly entered the reception area. Too late to renege. Gerri had paid for my incarceration in advance.

The six-hour drive had been peppered with bits and pieces of her own rehab experience at Chit-Chat three years prior. And punctuated in my mind by those heartbreaking flashbacks of Luke's trip.

In May of that same year, we delivered my oldest son, Luke to that same drug and alcohol program where my sister, Gerri had sobered up. Luke's first twelve days were spent in detox. At age twenty-eight, addiction had already robbed Luke of fourteen years of his life.

Beaten down by guilt and a sinking feeling of powerlessness over his disease, I finally surrendered to the fact that I needed help, too. It was the last thing I wanted to do, but I had to—for Luke. So when Gerri and her husband threw me a lifeline by offering to pay for a week of intensive therapy in the co-dependency program, I grabbed hold.

Unlike Gerri, who had actively sought out help for her drinking, I was there for a different reason—and for a much briefer period of time. My treatment plan was one that was designed to help those who were adversely affected by a loved one's addiction.

But I had mixed feelings about therapy.

My initial induction came once again at the hands of my sister. After thirty days of abstinence and what she referred to as the unraveling of her denial, she dove head first into recovery. She joined AA, searched out an Adult Children of Alcoholics group in our area, and dragged me along to every meeting, kicking and screaming. Admitting that my father, *my hero*, might be an alcoholic labeled me as a traitor. *How could I even entertain such a notion?*

Gerri seemed not to care about my feelings. Her only goal was to get on with her life and recover from her own addiction. I didn't blame her, but I also didn't share her enthusiasm.

Perspectives

Guilt spun its web of broken threads
Tangled me in misconceptions,
To label my dad an alcoholic
Tasted bitter—spelled deception.

Dad didn't sleep beneath a bridge
Or shirk his duties as assigned,
He gifted us with values
And never voiced a thought unkind.

Clad in love that wasn't frayed
We never went without,
He was nothing like the guy next door
Who drank all day till he passed out.

An alcoholic, in my mind,
Was an embarrassment and flawed,
Incapable of pulling off
This family-man façade;
Uncaring and abusive,
He would stagger, curse and shout.
His appearance and environment
Would prove beyond a doubt,
That here's a prime example
Of what a drunk is all about.

I couldn't grasp the concept,
Nor admit and then accept,
That alcoholism's a *disease*
Infecting those we least expect.

Yet here I was, on the doorstep of what was beginning to feel like our family Alma Mater, about to subject myself to the torture of exhuming all of the pain I had been trying to tap-dance around for years. *Something told me I was about to be skinned alive.*

I slipped into my cool and collected persona for the intake, but I was sweating bullets and Gerri knew it. Once I was signed, sealed and delivered, Gerri took me by the hand and led me outside and around the back of the building. We followed a garden path to a small domed structure surrounded by rustic benches, tucked under and shaded by weeping willows. A sign posted to one of the trees welcomed us to *Serenity row.* Now that's a dichotomy; weeping willows and Serenity Row.

I was still clutching Gerri's hand. When we sat down, and I finally released it, she gave me a look that said *I'm the big sister here today.*

"This is the Chapel, Dallas," she said. "I thought a quick prayer here couldn't hurt."

I was in no position to argue with her. We sat in silence for what seemed like an eternity.

I was beginning to feel uncomfortable. When Gerri arose and took me by the hand, I reluctantly followed her lead, and we entered the chapel. It had been so long since I had been inside a church, I expected God to pierce the dark with lightening bolts. Feeling unworthy to be treading on foreign soil, I nudged Gerri into the nearest pew.

Gerri whispered in my ear, "Just pray for honesty, open-mindedness, and willingness." She squeezed my knee. "I know you may not think so now, but down the road, you will count this experience as one of your greatest blessings."

God, I prayed she was right.

I knew I had at least scratched the surface of those

9

lofty goals the day I filled out the family history form relating to alcohol usage. That was the first time I took a serious look at how many members were wrapped up in its tentacles. Jumping off the pages were images of my father, a grandfather I had never known, my sister, my mother's sister, and my oldest son. No elbow room here for denial. A flood of unpleasant memories groomed in ugly incidents, nasty accusations, and numerous arguments—all involving alcohol—washed over me. This was my family, the people I loved, how could this be?

I felt like I was flailing around in a festering pool of toxic sadness without any floaties. Could this place possibly rescue me?

In the beginning, my knee-jerk reaction was, *this sucks.* Nothing new here. I felt just as alienated and estranged from everyone else as I always did in any kind of social situation. A fancy, renowned rehab sure as hell wasn't going to change that.

Orientation was a bit strange. They divided us up into smaller pods of seven or eight. We were as diverse a lot as members of the United Nations. They threw me in with a nurse; a dentist, who was an elderly man that oozed refinement and money; a female college student; a housewife; a teacher and an abused wife of a rageaholic. I wasn't quite sure where I fit into this conglomeration. Other than the fact that we all shared the common bond of either living with or being closely related to an alcoholic, we seemed to have little else in common.

We were quickly apprised of the house rules: No smoking; be prompt for meals; take turns at cleaning up and lights out at 10:00 p.m. We were then given explicit instructions by the therapists who would be facilitating our peculiar little group on the protocol for group *interaction*.

That ugly word—intense—kept bouncing off the walls

of my apprehension. I wanted to bolt. Why the hell did I let Gerri talk me into this? To top it all off, at the end of the session, a photographer was brought in to capture the varying degrees of misery behind our masked bravado.

The therapists had all kinds of innovative tools up their sleeves. They ran the gamut from forced sharing in the group; to writing letters to someone or something we were afraid to confront; to role playing. And last but not least, they gave us instructions on learning how to give and receive affirmations.

Recovery of any kind is not for sissies. I didn't realize it at the time, but it takes courage and a leap of faith not to bolt and run for higher ground. I was often tempted during that week to throw in the towel. The bruised forty-five-year-old child who filled out that form before stepping through the entrance door would have done exactly that.

Retrospect is the catalyst for truth. But one must be able to look back on reality from a rather detached perspective; the unvarnished version. For me, that took everything Chit-Chat had to offer.

The first day, while I was still wavering back and forth about whether I belonged there, three words printed on a chart hanging on the wall vanquished all doubt. It was a list of ten losses experienced by both the alcoholic and the co-dependent.

I skimmed over most on the list, allowing for several question marks; loss of pride, loss of hope, loss of faith, etc. But when it came to number ten, I crumbled**: Loss of spirit.**

There it was. The vast emptiness that had enveloped me all of my life, reduced to four syllables and tossed about for all to see. What if the others noticed that I stood accused? How dare they rip away my 'I'm okay' mask and leave me exposed.

There was a hole in the dike. My vision was blurred by that one small eruption in an ocean of dammed up tears that I could no longer force back. *Yes, I belonged here.*

Loss of Spirit

Erased?
Maybe…
by life,
by being discounted,
by alcohol-isms?

Or…
diffused and deleted
while inside the womb—
before cognition;
siphoned
thru heredity's placenta?

A dilemma of dodging answers
in between
the lines not rendered.

Was it ever there to be retrieved,
or is it simply nonexistent?
And if indeed that be the case,
my grief weighs more insistent.

But perhaps another option
tucked in hope's horizon
whispers;
recreate me my spirit pleads,
lest your white flag
makes me wither.

Opening the door and letting the monster out to roam the corridors of my misconceptions was nothing short of terrifying. I remember wondering as we shared our stories in the group of whether or not everyone was totally honest. I seemed to be the only one drowning in three generations of alcoholism.

In that one short week, my perceptions about the disease of alcoholism were shattered and reconstructed from the ground up. The educational part went down the gullet rather easily. It was like sipping cough syrup through a cherry-flavored straw and realizing it was medicinal; it couldn't hurt me because it was absorbed intellectually.

But rubbing elbows with the emotional devastation that rips across the fabric of family unity and shreds it to pieces—that wasn't going down without a fight. I in spite of my denial, the mask was stripped away and the misery that lurked beneath it was dressed in my pain; a pain denied for too many long years. It scraped the surface of my resistance like nails on a chalkboard, screaming to be released.

God, I needed a drink.

The Awakening

Truth unravels of its own accord
Exposing pain yet unexplored.

Doesn't matter if we're unprepared
Or beg of it, so we might be spared;

Truth rips away our worn-out shield
Points to where we now must yield.

I will not harm you, truth reveals
Embrace me, take the hand that heals.

13

I had so much to learn.

My earliest concept of an alcoholic was Bud Jarvis, our next door neighbor. Every weekend, Bud would sit on his stoop with his homemade wine camouflaged in a greasy-looking paper bag and drink until he became incoherent. Never did figure out the paper bag.

During the week, Bud was stone-cold sober and went to work every day. I always thought it strange that Dad sympathized with him. "You have to give him credit," he used to say. "He never misses a day's work."

At six years old, the concept of that dichotomy was a real disconnect. All I saw was an embarrassment to his children and a thorn in his wife's side. Mary Jarvis would scream and rant all day, and their kids fled next door to our house. Jimmy masked his shame behind a boisterous laugh while his brother Ray attempted to rub away the nervous twitch in his left eye.

I remember thinking that Bud should drink with Dad and the other guys in the neighborhood down at the corner bar. Then, maybe he wouldn't get so drunk.

The Corner Bar

Relief from stress back in the day
Was bottled or on tap,

It magnified the moment,
Helped fill in lack's growing gap.

The working stiffs who filled the stools
At the corner bar each day,

Would tip their glass and toast their dreams,
Then swallow them away.

When Luke gave his first lead at an AA speaker meeting, I didn't know what to expect. But he nailed it. I'm not sure who was more anxious. Him, because it was his first lead and his mother was in the room, or me because I was anxious about what might be revealed. It was kind of like watching a scary movie as a child and holding my hands over my eyes, but still peeking through the cracks. His very first sentence said it all.

"Hi, I'm Luke, and I am an alcoholic." He looked directly at me. "And if you shake our family tree, every kind of alcoholic you can imagine will come tumbling out."

Alcoholism's legacy is bestowed on random victims. There is no common thread. Genetics plays a part; like most other diseases, there is a predisposition. The environment is often a factor, but not a determining one. It targets people from all walks of life; young and old; rich and poor; uneducated, and drunks with doctorates. It doesn't favor A type personalities over B types, and it is blind to gender. There are binge drinkers; blackout drinkers; maintenance drinkers; those who like to call themselves functional drinkers, and low-bottom drunks who end up as wet brains.

From the onset, Luke had little defense against the disease. His progression was rapid. By the time he left home at eighteen, he was already a blackout drinker. Unlike Gerri and I, who were functional, *for the most part,* and dad, who managed to maintain a sober persona via a few shots and a six pack a day, Luke went from 0 to 10 in a few short years. Hell donned the label addiction, and raked him over the coals, taking him on a ten-year roller coaster ride before it dropped him, maimed and broken, on the doorstep of recovery at age twenty-eight.

Our Gene Pool

Lurking behind that initial high
Often undetected—
Our rebel gene would spin its web
Till generations were affected.

Its tentacles reached far and wide
Consuming young and old alike,
Its puncture wounds bled shame and guilt,
Threatening to breach the dike.

Our combined regrets bear out the fact
That our story when dissected,
Reveals a truth that if denied
Can never be corrected.

A host of other ailments
Wear that word *pre-disposition*,
But none demands recovery,
Shuck denial as its one condition.

A few days into the program. I was gaining an understanding of how being raised in an alcoholic home affected much of my behaviors. I learned that Gerri and I had developed an arsenal of defense mechanisms to cope. I also discovered that children of alcoholics assume specific roles in the family structure.

****

Sharon Wegsheider-Cruse developed a theory of alcoholic families which states that the children in such families tend to assume one of four roles.*

"The Family Hero" - This child brings esteem to the family through his or her achievements during the school years, such as being on the football team, the debate team, class president, the honor roll, the cheerleading squad, etc. This child may have decided long ago that he or she is maltreated by the alcoholic parent because they think "I'm not good enough" (which the parent often tells the child when angry or upset). So, to try to win the parent's love, the child becomes a super-achiever. An added benefit of being the Family Hero is that it gets you out of the house a lot and away from the family.

"The Scapegoat" - This child takes the other approach to the problem of why the alcoholic parent mistreats him or her, which is "I'm *not* good enough, so why not be really bad?" This is the child who argues, lies, steals, joins a gang, takes drugs, gets pregnant as a teen, runs away, etc. Within the family system, this child's behavior problems serve a useful function. He/she takes everyone's focus off of the marital conflict or the alcoholic's drinking and places it on them. Often the parents appear to be closer and more united while they cope with the constant crises this child creates. Also, this child "acts out" the anger other family members feel, but are unable to express.

"The Lost Child" - This quiet, passive child spends a lot of time in fantasy activities, playing, daydreaming, etc. He or she will often have minimal contact with other family members, although they are usually at home because this child withdraws into a shell to be protected from the anger and conflict often present in the home. The mother of such a child will often state, "I wish I had three more just like him/her" because this child does not make waves or make many demands on the parents' time or attention.

"The Mascot" - Is often the youngest child in the family. The mascot's role is to play the family clown. Their purpose is to bring laughter and fun into the home. They develop a dire need for approval from others and are viewed as the most fragile and vulnerable. Their behaviors are an act of defense against feelings of anxiety and inadequacy. As adults they may self-medicate with alcohol and/or tranquilizers.

*Excerpt taken from the book, *UNDERSTANDING CO-DEPENENCY (the Science Behind It and How Break the Cycle)* by Sharon Wegscheider-Cruse and Joseph Cruse, MD Health Communications, Deerfield Beach, Florida.

I wasn't quite sure where I fit, but since I was always being blamed for everything, scapegoat seemed a good fit. I had no problem labeling my sister Gerri. Although she saw herself as the *lost child*, she definitely incorporated the characteristics of *the hero.* Her perfectionism and people-pleasing attributes had made her life much more difficult than it needed to be.

One of the most profound revelations that opened my eyes to see just exactly where my sister and I fit in all the craziness was during a role-playing session. The scene was to portray an argument transpiring between my mother and father. I was asked to place my sister and myself in positions relating to the situation. I curled Gerri up into a ball and put her in a corner where she remained a coward, covering her face. I, on the other hand, was standing on a chair, smack dab in the middle of them, trying to keep the peace.

My sister was right. Back then, she was the lost child. But as she got a bit older, she developed her survival skills and transitioned into a super achiever and perfectionist. She *became* the hero. While I, on the other hand, honed my peacekeeping skills, always in the middle persona, and failed to move beyond it. I spent my entire life trying to fix everybody and everything that went wrong. *After all, it was probably my fault in the first place.*

Claudia Black, who has worked for forty years with children who live with alcoholism, believes that children of alcoholics learn three basic rules of life that help them survive in an alcoholic family: Don't Talk; Don't Trust; Don't Feel.

Not only did I hone these skills, but I wore them as a badge of courage.

****

As the week progressed, there was an almost imperceptible shift in the therapy sessions. By the time I realized it, it was too late to crawl back into my shell. The textbook educational information about the disease and its residual effects on the family had morphed into one ugly ball of wax that had my name written all over it. And it was gathering momentum as it rolled down my own mountain of pain.

I found myself sharing things that were so deeply buried that I didn't even have a name for them. Who was this stranger purging her innermost secrets in front of total strangers?

I was a good girl, never caused any trouble. What was so strange about a child banging her head up against the wall, or breaking dishes over her head? And so what if she sat in a corner and tried to look sad so someone would pay attention to her? Who says out of body experiences and the illusion of shrinking till the ones you love are no longer within your grasp isn't natural? *Sad little girl.*

The Burial

I buried my child
At a tender young age,
I buried her
In every heartache.

I buried my child
Within the fresh open wounds,
In the folds
Of the guilt and the shame.

In the slights and the losses
In the unspoken grief,
In the depths
Of my own isolation.

And the loose, porous soil
Mounted higher and higher,
As the strike of the shovel
Resounded.

And she delved so deep
With a fervor she burrowed,
Just how deep
Dared the little child go?

She sunk to the innermost
Chamber of self,
To a crypt
Where she felt protection—

From a world
Out of reach
Out of touch
Just beyond
The grave of her own isolation.

That behavior of piling hurt upon hurt until it reached the boiling point had followed me into adulthood. I spent years honing my skills and became quite creative. I toned down the violence and resorted to more precise ways to release all of the crap that I had never learned to deal with over the years. It manifested itself in scenes of me hiding in the closet and methodically taking scissors to my wedding dress; to tossing hot spaghetti on the ceiling, one f#*@-ing noodle at a time; to shutting myself in the bathroom and slowly releasing the gas in the antiquated space heater without using a match to ignite it. The preferred scenario was that my lying, cheating husband would realize how much he hurt me and break down the door to save me. (He never did.) And of course, I shut it off before becoming asphyxiated. Not exactly grown-up behaviors.

As an alcoholic, I began to use alcohol as a tool to avoid coping with life and stopped growing emotionally. My capacity to learn how to resolve issues became diminished.

Diminished

Diminished
the ability to absorb reality

Diminished
the desire to achieve

Diminished
the capacity to care for self and others

Diminished
the seal of self-respect

Diminished
the language of laughter

Diminished
the season of spirit

Diminished
All honor and hope.

By day four, I was willing to accept the fact that my childhood response to life was influenced by my dad's drinking and Mom's obsession to control it. Those dynamics caused many of my sister's and my needs to be ignored, so I compensated the best I could. But why hadn't I evolved?

Wrong question.

Before I left group that afternoon, one of my favorite counselors—one I trusted implicitly—asked me to stay behind.

"Dallas." She made a point to make eye contact. "This evening, I'd like for you to review your family history again. And this time, I want you to include your own drinking patterns. If you feel comfortable about it, I would like you to share it with me and the others tomorrow."

I was stunned. But being the people pleaser that I was, I couldn't refuse. Anyhow, I was sure my refusal would indict me. My drinking wasn't that bad, and I'd prove it.

After dinner, I went to my room, turned on the overhead fan, and pulled out a notebook. The thought of an ice cold beer flitted across my radar. But I sluffed it off, giving it little credence, and dove into the family tree.

I didn't know my dad's father. He died when I was a baby. To hear my dad tell it, Grandpa was a mean son of a bitch, a rageaholic who when he drank made life hell for my grandmother and everyone else. My earliest recollection of Grandma was that of a saint, lacking only the wings. She never complained, and if she had suffered any abuse at his hands, she kept it to herself. She radiated love and kindness toward everyone in her limited world.

It wasn't until my dad's brother died and my aunt brought us some of Grandma's memorabilia that I realized just how desperate she must have been. Tucked away in her Bible were old newspaper clippings articulating the work of the Washingtonians; a group dedicated to aiding alcoholics. That group was the forerunner to Alcoholics Anonymous.

Dad had four siblings; three brothers and a sister. To my knowledge, the only two who drank were Dad and Uncle

Gene. By far, they were the kindest and most gentle of the whole lot. As a young child of eight, I was genuinely aware of that fact. In all probability, it was a result of eavesdropping on adult conversations.

We rarely saw Uncle Carl. He was the oldest and rumored to be the most successful. He was a draftsman that at some point in his career had declined an offer to sign on with Walt Disney before Disney became famous. Uncle Carl lived in California, clear across the country, and rarely made it home.

Later on, my impression of Uncle Carl was that he was ashamed of his humble beginnings and preferred to distance himself both geographically and emotionally. Although he wasn't unkind, he was rigid, quite proper and aloof; a textbook example of the oldest sibling of an adult child of an alcoholic.

They all had their issues.

Next in line was Uncle Ralph. He lived nearby but was reclusive, suspicious of most people to the point of paranoia, and extremely introverted.

Aunt Selma suffered from chronic depression and committed suicide.

Uncle Gene lived a few hundred miles away, and I only remember him visiting us a few times so I'm not sure how excessive his drinking was. But he always had a cold beer in his hand while Aunt Dorothy hovered over him, keeping count.

That rageaholic alcoholic environment marked all of them in one way or another.

Family Dysfunction

Dysfunction breeds and festers
In the cauldron of addiction

It casts a net of broken dreams
Claiming family jurisdiction.

Behaviors often go unrecognized
Clues lie dormant for a while
Until another victim's life unfolds
In fates of alcoholic bile.

Mom was raised with an addiction just as devastating as alcoholism. Her father, Grandpap Allen, was a compulsive gambler. He was an affable Irishman with a big smile and the proverbial line of bullshit required of his occupation. Mom used to say that Grandpap could sell a refrigerator to the devil if he could get his foot in the door. He was a traveling salesman, and for a time, I guess, did quite well at it. But that was when Mom was young, and life was still good.

Gerri and I loved him. We spent many a weekend with him and Grandma Allen so Mom and Dad could get a break, *whatever that meant.*

For a long time, I didn't understand Mom's animosity toward him. Everything he said or did seemed to anger her. Later, I came to realize that our adulation of him was a powerful trigger for her. He had let his own children down, time and time again.

Due to his gambling, my grandfather had lost a brand new home, a string of jobs and several cars. When the bottom fell out, they moved from Ironton, Ohio to West Virginia and were forced to adapt to an entirely different lifestyle. On more than one occasion, Mom would come home from school and find them sitting on the steps, suitcases in hand. They had been evicted again for non-payment of rent.

Mom was the youngest of three siblings. Uncle John was ten years older and Aunt Mimi was two years behind John. The character traits and problems that the three of them inherited from that dysfunctional environment were similar to adult children of alcoholics.

Uncle John, like my dad's oldest sibling, got the hell out and stayed away, except for an occasional visit and telephone calls to make sure all was okay and no one was in dire need. Uncle John affected me as a very straight-laced, humorless perfectionist. He always seemed uptight, but he was a successful husband and father. I learned from his daughter just a couple of years ago—we reconnected after five decades—that he never discussed his upbringing with her or her two brothers.

Mom's sister, big Aunt Mimi, was what is referred to as a low-bottom drunk. Not only did she go as far down the ladder as feasible, but she lived there for the last fifteen years of her life. The fact that physiologically, the human body can sustain for years the kind of abuse and neglect that alcohol doles out was a hard lesson to swallow. Death would have been a blessing.

Mom and Dad entertained family every holiday. Up until the time Aunt Mimi became argumentative and started falling down steps, she was part of all of our celebrations. When Mom finally wrote her off, Gerri and I were appalled. Later, I realized she couldn't watch it anymore. She had repeatedly tried to talk her into seeking help, but to no avail.

Gerri and I attempted to keep in touch with big Aunt Mimi over her declining years. What we evidenced was heart-breaking. We never knew what we were going to find when we visited.

Aunt Mimi had taken up with people who were scamming her. On the pretext of bringing her food and checking on her, they would take her to the bank to cash her social security checks, buy her a couple of fifths and a handful of canned goods, and disappear until the next month. Sometimes the scammers who had no place else to go would be camped out in her living room for days on end. To this day, every time I think of her, that image of an old lady dressed in a moth-eaten mouton coat and a dirty pair of gloves cut out at the knuckles lying in a soiled bed with an open bottle of whiskey sitting beneath it over-rides whoever else she may have been. **And when I hear that term low-bottom, high-bottom, drunk, I am reminded that the only thing separating them is the word 'yet'.**

On her seventy-ninth birthday, the last one Gerri and I acknowledged, we took her a birthday gift. It was February 14th, Valentines day. That winter had been extremely cold. When we knocked on the door, we couldn't rouse her so we went around the side of the house to the entrance near her bedroom and tried to get in. The door was frozen shut. Her gas had been disconnected for non-payment. She remained antagonistic and wanted nothing to do with leaving that apartment. Our only alternative would have been to commit her, which we chose not to do.

Three years later in her eighty-third year, we received a call that she was in the hospital on life support. My mother refused to go. Gerri and I gathered our mixed bag of old memories, apprehensions, and lingering sense of duty and paid our final visit. The sound of the respirator managed to over-ride the drumming of our accelerated heartbeats, and at the same time, silenced our unspoken relief.

The next day as we struggled over the option to assume the responsibility of pulling the plug, her Higher Power interceded, setting her free at last.

Amber Liquid

At dawn the dew was shed like tears
Down the dirty window pane,

27

To cleanse the film of sorrow
That engulfed what now remained.

She lay stretched out in loneliness
Beneath a soiled and tattered sheet,
While visions of a wasted life
Would rewind, just to repeat.

On the floor, a dark brown bottle
Her companion all those years,
Spilled out its amber liquid
No escape now to drown her fears.

In the end, it had betrayed her
Stole those who cared away,
Death held peace, the only blessing
That relieved her on that day.

****

Sentence by sentence, as I put pen to paper on my family tree, my naivety was being stripped away. The ramifications this horrible disease had on our family was earth shattering.

Because my father was my hero, looking at his addiction through a lens that excluded delusion was devastating. I had always blamed Mom for all of the upheavals. When Mom gave him hell for spending too much time at the corner bar, I was the first to jump to his defense. *No wonder he drank, who wouldn't if they had to live with her constant nagging?*

Over the years, that skewed perception, reinforced by her co-dependent response to his drinking, forged an ever widening fissure in our fragile mother-daughter relationship.

Her need to control his drinking was tangled up with all of those fears and uncertainties overflowing from her own dysfunctional background. Combine that with obsessive compulsive disorder, an inferiority complex hiding beneath a Ceasar complex, and BOOM, welcome to my world; a world where confusion and inconsistencies reigned.

Mom was a workaholic, driven by perfectionism. She held down a full-time job, provided home-cooked meals, kept a spotless home, and spent endless hours dressing up her fear and frustration by excelling at all of them. She didn't have time to bother with foolish notions like relaxing, horsing around, or simply chatting for the sake of chatting.

Dad, on the other hand, was self-employed. He was an exterminator. Many of his small contracts were bars that required his services after hours. A perfect setup for a guy who liked boiler-makers (a shot of whiskey, chased by beer). Even in between the beer-joint hours he always had time to listen to our day, discuss frivolous ideas, and laugh. A luxury Mom apparently could not afford.

While Mom was painting the perfect picture, Dad was relaxing at the bar and giving us periodic emotional support. I probably loved my mom, but I never liked her. Her insecurities manifested themselves in what I found to be ugly traits. She elevated herself by constantly criticizing others; neighbors, co-workers, and even relatives. One of my greatest fears growing up was that she was probably pounding somebody else's eardrums.

She placed each and every male boss she ever had on the same pedestal where they were constantly praised, (at our dinner table) for the one quality that my dad lacked; ambition.

When Dad had one too many drinks, he usually became even more mellow. Except that is, when he became depressed and threatened to walk the railroad tracks, striking the fear in all of us that he was thinking about committing suicide. Or, when he revealed a side of himself that both shocked and scared my sister and me half to death.

Those were the times Mom never knew when to quit. She would strut right up to his six-foot frame, all four foot eleven of her, and rant and rave until he would push or slap her. As much as I loved Dad, on those occasions, my sympathy was with her.

My sister and I learned that approaching holidays meant that an imminent threat lurked on the horizon. The anticipation of fun and all of the preparation was usually marred by Dad's need to start celebrating at Vern's Bar a few days ahead of time.

Sundays were family days. And unless it rained, we hiked to Nichol's Hill. Mom would carefully pack a picnic basket brimming with homemade goodies that she and Dad would take turns pulling in a wagon. Gerri and I filled our knapsacks with the paper products, table cloth, and a blanket. Then off we would go.

It was about a four-mile trek, punctuated with about a mile and a half of hilly terrain. Some days the heat was relentless, and in between the huffing and puffing, Gerri and I would be moaning and groaning under our breath. But once we reached the spring and spread our blanket, Mom poured everyone a cold iced tea from the thermos and the discomfort fell away in the shade of a lazy afternoon filled with games, fried chicken, and best of all, fun and laughter. Those were perfect days…until we made our routine pit stop at Red Hanks on the way home.

Red Hanks was another neighborhood beer-joint (back then there was one on every corner). There was Vern's, the closest and most frequented; a heavily trafficked set of concrete steps paved the way to the Alvan on McColloch Street, and three doors down from that place was Snyders.

We were on a first-name basis with the owners and all of the regulars.

Each bar had its own significance. Vern's was the closest and where Dad did most of his alone time drinking. It was the crux of most of Mom and Dad's troubles. Mom did not like being left out, but more importantly, it was impossible to control his alcohol intake from behind the switchboard at the hospital where she worked shifts.

Then there were those two incidents that probably justified her concern. Because of its proximity, Dad felt secure in the fact that we would fare okay if he slipped off for a few while we were in his charge. How much trouble could we get into? We were good kids, right?

It didn't happen often, but one day my sister and I got into a big fight. I tried to stop Gerri from bothering Mom at work and worrying her. I even agreed to put the knife down, if she would do the same with the scissors. But I was unsuccessful. Mom left her job and was home within half an hour, fuming at us, and Dad, for leaving us alone. Nobody got hurt. Back then, I couldn't wrap my head around why she made such a big deal about it. That argument went on for over a week.

Now the slashed wrist incident, that was a different story.

Gerri and I were goofing off. We did that a lot when we were unsupervised. Dad stopped for a few, and Mom was working afternoons. It was all in fun. Gerri was out on the patio, and just as she came barreling toward me, I slammed the back door shut, and her arm went crashing through the glass pane. Blood squirted everywhere.

Alarmed, frightened, and knowing we were in trouble, I wrapped the gushing wound and decided to call Dad at Verns. It required five stitches. We were eight and ten years old. Guess Mom had a point after all.

The Alvan and Snyders tended to be family affairs. They

31

both had good food, bowling machines, and a host of other kids whose parents, like ours, were seeking a few hours relief from the tedium of their work week. I could always bank on the fact that I would run into my best friend, Gina, at one of these fine establishments.

Poor Gina. I always wondered if she was embarrassed by her parents. It never failed. As the evening wore on and the booze kept flowing, they would become boisterous and crude. A vicious argument would always ensue. Thank God, my parents didn't behave like that. I remember thinking, *They must be alcoholics.*

Red Hanks, the bar at the top of the hill where we capped off our Sunday picnics was the one my sister and I both hated. It was a blemish on an otherwise perfect day. To begin with, we didn't know any of the kids. It was located in the projects, a place where we were not permitted to play, even though it was just around the corner from where we lived. The kids didn't like us and we didn't like them.

We would arrive around 6:00 p.m; be sent outside to play until dusk, then go back inside and languish in our boredom while Mom and Dad continued to order over and over again one more beer. Resting our heads on the table, or falling asleep, invited a swift nudge under the table to the shins. It was usually during Boston Blackie, a detective series that aired at 10 p.m. when we trekked on home.

Monday mornings were *"Up and at em, kids, it's a school day."*

Our parents were good, hard-working people who did their best. We may have been poor, but we always had a roof over our heads, home-cooked meals, and decent clothes on our back. We never doubted for a minute that we were loved, but the alcohol problem had a way of snaking its contradictions into the fabric of our lives.

Periodically, when the shit would hit the fan and Mom

would threaten to leave, Dad would quit. Sometimes it would last for months at a time. Things would improve, the fighting would cease, and Dad would attack home improvement tasks with gusto—there was that ambition Mom was always talking about. It was there all along, hiding inside the Black Label bottle. Mom was easier to live with, and the tension that furrowed her brow and pursed her lips began to relax.

Then bang, without warning, the rug was ripped out from under us. The magic carpet ride was over.

Over the years, the cycle continued. I could never figure out what triggered these relapses, but I did recognize the fact that it always began with the mindset that he could stop at the corner for just one beer. Just one always led to another and another.

The length in between drinks didn't matter. Alcoholism is a progressive disease. Little did any of us know at the time, that it is the engine, not the caboose, that runs you over. The word alcoholic was never bandied about in our home. No one really understood the disease or the various ways it manifested itself. It remained disguised for years until some of us trickled into recovery.

Addiction (an Acrostic poem)

Adverse reaction to chemicals
Disguised in fermented fantasies
Dreams defaced in alleyways
Incentive evicted, room for rent
Crystal conveys new images—
Traces of meth in rotting teeth
Isolation creeping closer
Orange jumpsuits carry jacked-up price tag
Nothing to salvage, sobriety shot.

Dallas H

****

By midnight, I was worn out. All I wanted to do was turn down the static and bury myself under my blanket of denial. But I still had a mountain of crap to unearth. My own, as well as Luke's usage, was weighing heavy on my heart. Luke's alcoholism couldn't be denied. But the guilt that I had been lugging around for failing to recognize and address it was going to be a huge hurdle. As for my own romance with alcohol, I had a gnawing suspicion that what was about to be revealed would rob me of my delusion. Chit-Chat was threatening to put the cap on my escape hatch.

My Story

I was never comfortable in my own skin. People and social interaction threw me into a tailspin. As early as the first grade, I felt disconnected from myself, as well as from others. Feeling *inadequate* and *less than* were mainstay emotions that followed me everywhere. They were my constant companions for years. I sensed early on that this wasn't normal. I needed to camouflage it so I wouldn't be pointed out as *God forbid, different than my peers.* So I adapted by becoming a chameleon. This was my initial journey into compromising myself. I could be anything you wanted me to be. I could look like you, talk like you, and in each and every aspect of this charade, appear normal. I became so adept at it that no one would ever suspect that deep inside I was registering a seven on the Richter scale.

Since alcohol was a staple in our family, it held no strange fascination for Gerri and me. It was simply a dessert choice on life's menu. In the beginning, it was never the main entrée. Growing up, we were never served it; we knew it

34

was reserved for adults. But that didn't stop us from licking the head off an ice-cold beer or sneaking a taste of the red bubbly stuff served in the gold-rimmed goblets on special occasions.

In a hurry to be emancipated, I married at sixteen. Two and a half years and two babies later, I had acquired a new friend. It came disguised in brown quart bottles, and on holidays when we could afford something fancier, it beckoned to me in decorated decanters. Alcohol provided me one critical coping tool. One that I used to survive a twenty-two-year hostage situation otherwise referred to as a marriage. It provided me with an avenue of escape; at least in theory.

I had a high tolerance, and I tested it frequently. I could drink most of our friends under the table, including the men. I always thought a high tolerance was the earmark of a successful social drinker. It was the ones who couldn't hold their liquor that were destined for trouble! One of many fallacies that I subscribed to. In retrospect, the truth had a way of usurping a different shade of denial in every remembrance.

Early on, my drinking was limited to both opportunity and a tight budget. Family celebrations were enhanced by the thought of free-flowing booze. The probability that they might end in chaos as a result of that factor didn't matter. I just put that irritation on the back burner and drank it away. Monthly Bunco games, ladies night out, was another excuse to imbibe. We rotated turns hosting the games. The fact that I was the only one turning them into a drinking fest escaped me at the time.

Our first apartment was in a complex populated by young couples with children. On hot evenings, we would congregate outside, and I would usually provide the beer. Because money was scarce, I would sometimes load my son's oversized baby carriage with pop bottles and return them to the corner grocery store for refunds to buy that beer. I never gave that sight a second thought, it was a means to an end. I could unwind and *maybe* fit it. The weight of being the youngest and poorest of that group could be lifted with the twist of a cap.

I drank because...

Beginnings—
birthed in a family's womb
felt comfortable—protected,
the thought that any harm could come
oft simmered undetected.

Amongst
perceptions handed down,
engraved in tangled thinking
were fantasies embedded
in excuses spent on drinking.

I'm ill at ease—I don't fit in
It helps me to relax,
It certainly enhances
the way I play the sax;

The pain's too great—
my nerves are shot,
let's celebrate
the day's so hot.

I work so hard, I need a break
bring on the wine, forget the steak;
I feel depressed, I need that buzz
the reasoning is *just because.*

They sounded like good reasons
and made perfect sense to me
till my future found me flailing
lost in alcohol's Dead Sea.

Drinking to fit in and overcome my feelings of inferiority were superseded by an obsessive need to escape life in general and to medicate the emotional pain of being in an abusive marriage. As my drinking progressed, it took on a life of its own. I learned that I could use alcohol to alter my moods, bury the truth, or just mentally check out. If I shuffled the beer, wine, and hard liquor around, I could master the Universe.

I found the false courage to stand up to a rageaholic husband in a shot glass. The thought of the repercussions that would follow for incurring his wrath never entered my mind. They were floating around in the bottom of my third or fourth bourbon and soda.

Socialization skills came in handy after my divorce when I was making the bar scene, and could be suctioned out of a bottle of Chablis or Chianti. It was nothing for me to saddle up to the bar once my tongue had been loosened and my brain put on hold to join strangers, horning into their conversations. While I was drinking, I loved intellectual debates. It wasn't too long before everyone disappeared to the other side. I had managed to argue them right off of their stools.

And I loved to dance. I can remember my ex-husband, Steve, telling me that booze and music would be my downfall. Once the band shifted into some funky get-down beat, and I had chugged enough alcohol to shed my introvert persona, I became a raging exhibitionist on the dance floor. I could keep up with the best of them. Suddenly, I was the center of attention, *especially those few times I took a spill.*

Essential Elixer

Alcohol
as it became essential
began erasing my potential;
it
released my inhibitions
in grinding dance-floor exhibitions;
it
striped away my last reserve,
loosed my tongue,
festooned me in flamboyant verve;
it
encouraged me
to place my trust
in liquid amber's fading dust.

****

After my divorce in '82, my drinking career really took off.
The two oldest of my kids, Luke and Jake, got out as fast as
they could. Luke was already on his way to near annihilation.
He moved down state and took a job as an assistant chef at
a hotel where he was given free room and board. And Jake,
at the ripe old age of nineteen, married his sixteen-year-old
sweetheart and joined the military. Nick and I were on our
own. The screaming and yelling came to an abrupt halt the
day Steve left. I remember thinking that with him out of the
picture, everything I touched would suddenly turn to gold
and life would be great.

Yet I continued drinking!

Looking back on my alcohol dependency with the
blinders off revealed some very pathetic behaviors. Leaving
my fourteen-year-old son at home alone until the wee hours

of the morning while I was out celebrating my new found independence suddenly seemed inexcusable. Laughing hysterically in the stall of a bathroom in an exclusive nightclub when I found myself unable to get up off the toilet seat because gravity kept pulling me backward; the restroom attendant didn't think that was particularly funny. And one of the images embedded in my heart forever; the devastating look of embrassement on Nick's face the night I bumped into his teacher at a fair and spilled beer all over her. In each of these instances, I was able to sluff it off. I was totally unaware of their improprieties.

But…here it comes the big but; the one syllable word for justification. I never had a DUI; never went to jail, seldom staggered, maybe slurred my words once in a while, and didn't drink in the mornings. Yes, I may have graduated into daily drinking over the last three years. But during the week I was able to limit it to only three or four beers. Just enough to take the edge off. Not exactly my idea of an alcoholic.

Flashback: An image of Gerri and I, dressed in *stress* after a grueling evening at our second job, pulling into the carry-out. Tom, a friend of Luke's, wearing that know-it-all grin would have the half gallon of Pink Chablis, our guaranteed stress reliever, already bagged and waiting. That went on for several months when Gerri and I worked for the magazine company.

When I married and left home, I hadn't realized that Gerri was devastated. I had left her alone to deal with Mom and Dad's carousel of alcoholic dysfunction. She developed serious abandonment issues that paved the way to her own addiction.

I was so wrapped up in my own journey that I wasn't aware of Gerri's problem until after my divorce when we moved in together. We both got our tickets to freedom within months of each other. Her youngest was a senior and decided to stay with his dad so he could finish out his last year of high school at John Marshall. Nick was the last of my three children still at home. Gerri moved in and together we drowned our miseries in twelve packs and gallons of wine.

During the day she taught, and I worked for a collection agency. We were both struggling financially so we supplemented our income telemarketing three nights a week. It was the lowest point in both our drinking careers. A fly-by-night company rented space from the collection aency where I was a supervisor. It was the perfect set up. The telephone and cubicles were already in place. The rental agreement had one stipulation; that I would be hired so I could oversee and protect the agency's interest.

Rule number one: No drinking in the building.

One week into the nightmare and I was sneaking in miniatures. People came and went faster than I could count them. We were selling $400 magazine contracts to people who couldn't afford a new pair of shoes, let alone four-year subscriptions to modern romance and sports periodicals. There was constant mental whip cracking disguised as cheerleading going on. Someone would troll behind the telemarketers snatching up sales that would then be turned over to a closer. Everyone that failed to close moved closer to their last paycheck. My nerves were shot. By day, I was dunning people for money and by night pushing them further into debt. That conflict would cause anyone to drink. Right?

Delusion always ruled my world. I saw myself as the perfect mother. I worked two jobs, kept a clean house, cooked real meals, and above all loved my children. That was the smoke screen I hid behind. Make it all look good on the outside and pretend those little guffaws would go unnoticed.

Every time I was confronted with a situation that required an action or decision, I reached for that magic elixer that relieved me of all responsibility. The fear of making a wrong decision was replaced by a fantasy that I so often ascribed to; *it will all be better tomorrow.*

The Marriage

For a while,
delusion
served me well,
delivered me from days of hell;
when
truth would rear its ugly head
I'd tip the bottle—kill it dead,
when
pricked by pain
or
fraught with fear,
I'd drown it in another beer.
When
life demanded courage
then
hard liquor quelled that call,
prompting me to shelve it
in the shadows where I'd crawl.
Once
delusion married alcohol
the two were intertwined,
impossible to separate—
a cancer spreading through my mind.
Reality'sassignment
doesn't grade one on charades
it reserves the stars
for lessons learned
untangling delusions' braids.

Most of my guilt concerning Luke's addiction was anchored to sins of omission, rather than commission. And it started before he ever picked up the first drink.

The tension in our home vacillated between thunderheads of simmering silence or lightning bolt rants. Steve used these tactics to keep everyone in line. We all lived in fear of the next explosion.

By the time Luke was twelve years old, he was looking for an escape hatch. I later learned that his drinking began around that age.

Steve was relentless in his verbal abuse. Luke and I bared the brunt of it. We were his targets. Luke couldn't ever do anything right. Steve ridiculed him at every opportunity shredding to pieces what little self-esteem Luke may have had. *What did I do about it?* I took another drink to drown that spreading cancer in my gut that said I should have stood up to Steve and protected my son. Jake and Nick escaped most of their father's wrath. They were left dangling out there on the periphery. There was no room in the cauldron for their emotional needs to rise to the surface. And I was too busy dodging the next bullet to notice.

The ability of a mind dependent on alcohol to cope with problems by simply eradicating the truth is incredible. When Luke was around fifteen, he started hanging out with an older crowd. Ones who had easy access to booze. They weren't bad kids, but they were well into their alcohol and drug addictions. I told myself different things to cope. Maybe they do drink too much, but at least Luke made a connection with friends who really cared about him and who he felt he could trust. I'd certainly proven that he couldn't trust me.

How bizarre is that? I had turned my son over to the care of alcoholics and addicts to give him the so-called nurturing that I couldn't. I justified it, because every time I questioned that reasoning, I could make it go away—obliterate it.

****

Exhausted at 3:00 a.m., I finally put the notebook down, called it quits and tried to go to sleep. A kaleidoscope of previously denied scenarios kept fluttering across the periphery of yesterday's mindset. I was morphing into something, but I wasn't sure exactly what. I tossed and turned during what remained of that tell-tale night, haunted by what the exercise had revealed.

The next day, following my purging, that same therapist who we fondly referred to as the Flying Nun dismissed the others and asked me to remain. I could sense a one-on-one discussion hovering in the works. I was okay with that. She didn't intimidate me. She impressed me as being the real thing. Unlike the ones who were always flapping their wings and spewing their holiness about when I attended St Joseph's High School.

This woman shared openly the details of her own downward spiral into addiction, and it resonated with me. If it could happen to a nun, I guess it could happen to anyone. It made my reality a little easier to swallow.

She threw me a cushion and motioned for me to join her on the floor. I sat down beside her, and she turned her pillow around so we were facing each other.

"Dallas, how did you feel about what you shared today?" she asked.

I began drumming my fingers on the hardwood floor. I didn't know what to say. Life, as I had always believed it to be, was coming apart at the seams. The proof was in the tear-stained journal. Yesterday's perceptions were being unraveled like a ball of yarn. The game was over. The horse was out of the gate, and I knew right then, there was no turning back.

I lifted my head and looked her dead in the eye. "Reality bites."

Claudia, that was her name, took my hand and preceded to tell me what I really didn't want to hear.

"I believe that somewhere, Dallas, and it doesn't matter when, that you have crossed that invisible line into alcoholic drinking."

I held her gaze, my lips quivering. The drumming became louder and more rapid. I knew exactly when it escalated. It was after the divorce. Luke and Jake, who were ten and eight years older than their brother, Nick, had escaped as soon as they turned eighteen. Suddenly, I saw my opportunity and seized it. I began hitting the bar scene every weekend, leaving Nick to fend for himself. He was almost fourteen, I rationalized, beyond needing a babysitter. My mom and dad lived right next door. He would be fine.

She grabbed my free hand and stilled it. "I think you should incorporate some AA meetings into your Adult Children recovery schedule.

She waited for a response, and when she didn't get it, she added, "As a matter of fact, I think AA should be your primary recovery program."

I spent the rest of the week clothed in an uncomfortable persona. I had entered the lion's den an innocent victim, and somehow, with the flip of a switch, I had become part of the pride; a threat to myself as well as to the ones I loved. It was a lot to assimilate, but with the help of the group and Claudia, an invisible weight lifted. Out of nowhere, tucked away inside the truth, a ray of hope began to materialize.

The week ground to a halt. Everyone gathered in the community room. As we spilled tears of relief and affection, we bid our counselors and each other goodbye. Addresses and telephone numbers were exchanged, along with fervent vows to keep in touch. The photographer took a curtain call and miraculously coaxed forth the joy reflected in the promise of new beginnings.

Suitcase in hand, I stood under the weeping willow and watched as Gerri turned the bend at the bottom of the hill. A flood of emotions fought their way to the surface. Fear of what lay ahead jockeyed with the joy of a second chance; love, faith, and the rebirth of spirit washed over me. But the overriding sentiment that rustled the breeze and invited the sunshine that day was the love and gratitude I felt for my sister. The first one in our family to break the mold and enter recovery.

****

I didn't know much about AA even though Gerri had been attending meetings for three years. It really wasn't a part of her life that I had been anxious to learn about. As a matter of fact, I felt a slight resentment. Thanks to AA I no longer had a drinking, partner. When Luke came home from Chit-Chat, I attended a few meetings to support him. My recollection was that they seemed to be a friendly group of people hooked on caffeine. And that was the extent of it. I was happy for him that it existed.

On the eve of my departure, I wrestled with it all; the disease itself; how it affected the formation of my character; the choices I either made or failed to make as a result and ultimately, my own drinking career. After wandering through the maze half of the night, I decided to take Claudia's advice and step into the ring. I was far from admitting I was an alcoholic, but it was something I needed to determine for myself. As long as no one applied any pressure, or I felt trapped, I'd give AA a chance.

Commitment was never my strong suite, but that night I

made one to myself. Thank God, no one, including Gerri, ever once pointed their finger at me and accused me of being an alcoholic. I was still in denial. When I walked through the doors of AA and proceeded, for many months, to introduce myself as an adult child of an alcoholic, I was offered a seat, warm smiles, handshakes and a cup of coffee.

Navigating Recovery

A ny fears I had about being indoctrinated into a group
think tank dissipated rather quickly. I attended about
four meetings a week, rarely spoke, sat in the back and
kept my distance. In time, I began to absorb the struggles
of others and realized that I wasn't alone, nor was I
unique. We shared the same fears; made many of the same
mistakes; and used alcohol to escape life, decisions, and
responsibilities.

Bit by bit my carefully constructed wall, built to keep
others out and to protect me, began to crumble. A crack
in the armor appeared and allowed me to navigate new
concepts to determine for myself whether or not I belonged
in the rooms of Alcoholics Anonymous.

Confusion reigned for several months. In the group
therapy meetings for Adult Children of Alcoholics, I
learned about the characteristics one develops to cope
with the dysfunction that prevails in alcoholic homes.
They taught me that it wasn't my fault. And above all, they
encouraged self-love and acceptance. The focus was to
build self-esteem and to be able to understand and identify
the cause of all the negative feelings and behaviors we had
developed over the years. This program, with a few slight
variations, was also a twelve step program.

Reclamation

Welcome to my childhood and all that it entails,
it's rooted in dysfunction, here're a few details:
We didn't get acquainted till I was middle-aged
then I thought it silly and so I disengaged.
Dressed in false maturity, I popped out of the womb
pretended I was all grown up, hid deep inside that tomb;
I chose responsibility instead of fun and laughter,
ignored the invitation of my peers and family forever after.
Environment and circumstance all played a vital part
to fan the flames that forced me to retreat into my heart.
Then along came alcohol, I opened it like a flower
until it crushed my petals and became my Higher Power.
I sacrificed adulthood to years of bad decisions
ones that couldn't manifest a childhood
without new provisions;
I wasn't sure who I was or what I really wanted,
but I approached recovery full speed ahead, undaunted.
Like the layers of an onion, my façade peeled away
that's when I heard her whisper,
I'm your child, come out and play.

My AA program was asking me to be accountable for my
own conduct, clean up my side of the street, put my energy
into taking a personal inventory and make amends to those I
may have harmed. Because I was so early in recovery, I had
yet to get a sponsor or work the steps. I couldn't weave all
of what seemed to be two different approaches to healing,
into one cozy quilt.

I became so conflicted that I decided to discontinue the
group therapy sessions until I could get better grounded in
sobriety.

It turned out to be a wise move because it wasn't until I came to terms with the addiction and all of its ramifications, that I became able to absorb and work the principals of both programs in order complete my tapestry of recovery.

My attitude and outlook were steadily improving. I was coming up on eight months sober. I had made several friends and no longer felt alcohol was the answer to all of my problems. But something was missing.

I began to feel as though I were stagnating.

I had put off asking anyone to be my sponsor. I was petrified of being rejected. But trying to work the program alone wasn't working. Asking for help was not in my nature. I was an independent, self-sufficient woman; another *glaring* characteristic.

No one in the program was pressuring me. They were quite content to let me flail about for as long as I needed.

Some of the common flaws weaved into the alcoholic personality are false pride and a lack of humility. Two traits I would have sworn did not apply to me. Anxious to prove it, I fluffed my peacock feathers, patted myself on the back and sought out a sponsor.

When the first one rejected me due to a conflict with her schedule, I licked my wounds, put my big-girl pants on, and continued the search.

Sponsorship was the discussion topic at many of the meetings I attended so I had a good idea of what it entailed. The sponsor's job is to guide you through the Twelve Steps and be available when needed. Many sponsor/ sponsee relationships go beyond that, developing into solid friendships. I wasn't sure that was what I was looking for. I found that idea to be a little intimidating.

It took me a few days to recover from my bruised ego, but I was determined to try again. Tenacity was one of my defining traits. Whether it was a virtue or a flaw depended on circumstance and interpretation. So after a Thursday night meeting, I approached my target.

Sara was nothing like me, *except* for the way she drank and her subsequent denial system. She was the poster-child for the term goody-two-shoes, the kind of person I would never have hung around with when I drank. I intuitively knew I had to have someone that I could not bullshit, and after listening to her share around the tables for months, she met that criterion.

The first thing out of my mouth, after I asked her, before the ink on the question mark was even dry, was that I couldn't stand to be told what to do. My knee-jerk response was to do exactly the opposite; authority figures rubbed me the wrong way.

Sara was expressionless. Without batting an eye, she held my defiant attitude in a long, tense pause. "Okay, we can give it a try and see if it works out."

I was having a hard time reading her. Was I on trial, or what? I was probably pushing my luck.

"Oh, one more thing," I said. "I know the telephone is supposed to be the favored tool of communication here, but I'm not very good at that. I work on the phone all day." I waited for a response. Nothing. So I continued, "Just trying to be honest!"

While the others filed out of the room, she gathered up the literature and handed me a plastic crate. "Here, you can help me clean up."

I thought I detected a hint of a smile.

"Then we can go to Ho Jo's for coffee." A definite smile. "Since you don't like talking on the telephone."

That was the first day of a twenty-eight-year-old relationship that changed my life. We became the Lone Ranger and Tonto, trekking off into unknown territory. I had so much to learn. Little did I know then that my guide was a drug and alcohol counselor. God works in mysterious ways.

We faced off every Thursday night after the meeting over coffee at Ho Jo's. Round one usually began with me dodging questions and tap-dancing around the issues, all the while maintaining eye contact. The way I saw it, avoidance had nothing to do with dishonesty. I was in awe of the fact that this kind, gentle, and respected woman could be an alcoholic.

One evening when I was feeling quite defensive, she struck me with, "It is a disease, you know. We aren't bad people trying to get good. We are sick people trying to get well."

There was some fancy footwork going on during those sessions. About four weeks into it, a subtle almost undetectable transition began to take place. I managed, once in a while, to pick up that two-ton telephone in between sessions. I found I was no longer so bent on defending my position that I couldn't hear the similarities as Sara unraveled her experiences involving alcohol.

Trust, especially of other women, was a hurdle I never expected to clear. Part of that hinged on my mother's and my strained relationship over the years. She had always been very critical of everything I did or didn't do, who I was, and who I wasn't. When the lesson is that you can't do anything right, guess what? You put the book down and quit trying.

So here I was, this wary drop-out, warming up on one of the toughest obstacle courses I had ever run.

Sara's training as a drug and alcohol counselor gave her an in-depth understanding of what she was dealing with as a sponsor. She was familiar with co-dependency, as well as the alcohol curse. She became my mentor and confidante. But the closer I got to the realization that I might be an alcoholic, the harder I fought it.

The Final Round: Shadowboxing

I was about eight months into the program when, in an attempt to disprove it, I made a list of all the reasons I couldn't be an alcoholic. Ater the Thursday night meeting, we headed to Ho Jo's. I was unusually quiet as we waited for the waitress to take our order. I knew it hadn't gone unnoticed.

Sara had a quizzical expression embedded in her question. "Is something wrong, Dallas?"

"No, not really." I wanted to wait until we were served. I didn't want any interruption when I proceeded with my litany.

When I couldn't stand the silence any longer, I reached into my pocket and pulled out the crumpled piece of paper from my jacket. "I need to read this to you, ok?"

She nodded her head yes, without saying a word, relaxed and became a deadly sounding-board.

"I've been tossing this around, and I wrote down why I don't think I am an alcoholic." Then I captioned it with, "Now, I might drink alcoholically, but that doesn't necessarily mean I am a real alcoholic."

1. Everyone needs to unwind.
   (alcohol's better than drugs, right?)
2. I still go to work every day. (Don't drink till evenings. Except on weekends.)

3. Always took care of my kids. (If I'm out drinking, I call Nick from the bar to check on him.)
4. Never had a DUI. (Only had a few minor accidents. It was icy when I ran into the church and knocked down the gutter.)
5. Only get really loaded on weekends. (Mom lives right next door if there is ever a problem.)

By the time I was halfway through, the echo bouncing off her silence was deafening. God how stupid it all sounded. I gave Sara a sheepish look, shrugged my shoulders, and realized there could be no retreating back into my fantasy world.

Neither of us said anything. She gave me a hug and we called it a night.

The following Thursday at the meeting when it came time for me to speak, I looked Sara in the eye and said without hesitation, "I'm Dallas, and I'm an alcoholic."

****

There may be other roads to recovery. Some find it in extended rehabs, others in religion, and there are those who attempt to achieve it with therapy alone. But for me, AA had a proven track record for those who were serious.

I learned how to pick up the two-ton telephone, and checked in with Sara of my own volition. Opening up to another woman was difficult; trust was an issue. I didn't seem to have any difficulty in sharing some of my drinking escapades, though. After all, I had heard worse around the tables.

But sharing my feelings, that was a different story. Half the time I couldn't identify them. If I were given a test on cash register honesty, I probably would have passed with flying colors. I didn't have a clue about self-honesty, about what I truly thought or felt. Those emotions were foreign to me, buried in some far off archeological site called childhood. And they needed to be excavated with the greatest of care. What if they were toxic and alienated everybody?

****

Everybody should be handed a brand new dictionary when they enter recovery. So many of the hard-learned concepts about life that we drag behind us have to be traded in for more positive, constructive ones.

Moving on, Sara suited up in her Tonto garb and began clearing away the brush. She dipped into her bag of tricks and attacked the overgrown tangles that stunted my progress. She spread a table of love, understanding, and acceptance and invited me to dine. She shuffled flashcards and affixed new insights into old beliefs embedded in the negativity that lurked in misguided perceptions, penned by myself and others in my old dictionary.

"What does surrender mean to you, Dallas?" Sara asked one day.

That was an easy one. "It means to give up, the other person wins." I continued on to say, "But that is something I don't do. When I was a kid, I loved playing tug of war. As a matter of fact, if there was an uneven number, I always chose the side with the least kids." I grinned. "I told you I was tough."

Sara was amused. "And where did that get you?"

I thought for a moment. "Well, sometimes it got me rope burns and skinned knees."

"In the program, sometimes surrendering is the very thing that makes us strong." Sara paused. "For instance, until we can resign ourselves to the fact that we *are* alcoholic, we can't recover."

I needed to mull that around for a while.

I found out that *gratitude* was more than just saying thank you, or spitting it out and then, later on, regretting it because you felt you were indebted to someone when they showed you a kindness.

And *humility* had nothing to do with shrinking from responsibility because you felt you couldn't do it perfectly. "We call that one ego, Dallas."

Did I say I had a lot to learn earlier?

I was moving forward, but it wasn't always painless. As the fog lifted, there were unpleasant memories lurking in the unvarnished truth. They were tucked away in pockets of yet-to-be-acknowledged regrets, released in sporadic flashbacks. They struck like bolts of lightning, and when I least expected it.

One Saturday morning, I was on my hands and knees scrubbing the kitchen floor when out of nowhere I began to feel shaky. I sat down in the middle of that chore and was suddenly catapulted back into an uglier Saturday morning.

I had been out drinking all night. But like the good little homemaker I professed to be, even though I didn't hit the bed until 5:00 a.m., I set the alarm for 7:00 so I could get up and continue my charade. Everything always had to look good to the outside world; one example of how the mind struggles to protect the disease.

I remembered having that same shaky feeling and bemoaning the fact that I couldn't crack open a beer for at least another hour. (It was a proven fact that only alcoholics drank before noon!) My anxiety and irritability were mounting by the minute. When Luke ventured downstairs to ask for breakfast, he had no idea he was about to step on a land mine. I verbally exploded all over him, then left him to his own devices to remove the shrapnel while I reached into the fridge and snapped the cap on the only thing that would bring me relief.

For lack of a better word, I used to call those episodes hang-overs. Everybody had them. Or did they? I began to wonder if they could have been withdrawal symptoms. Was the difference merely a word preference, or was my interpretation another notch in my well-honed system of denial. If I never got anything else perfect in my life, I had managed to whittle *denial* down to a fine art.

Thank God, I wasn't assaulted all at once with a barrage of my well-disguised crap. If I had been, I probably wouldn't have made it. There was a greater plan at work.

As I continued with Sara and began to feel safe in our relationship, little by little I became strong enough to recognize the truth as it was revealed to me in bits and pieces. This is the process of recovery.

One of the slogans in the AA program is **HOW.** It's an acronym for honesty, open-mindedness, and willingness. **HOW** worked backward for me. Early on, total honesty wasn't possible. I was still saturated with alcoholic thinking, shame, and guilt. Until I began to work through these issues and learned a little bit about the disease, it's ramifications, and the recovery process, for the most part, I remained blind to the truth.

But I was *willing*.

That is what allowed me to come into the rooms; strap myself in, take the cotton out of my ears, and begin to put aside my biases about alcoholism. Eventually, a small crack appeared in my thinking. And as that crack slowly *opened*, I found myself tuned in to a brand new radio station. I was receiving and assimilating the kind of support and information that would, with the help of a sponsor and the fellowship, unlock the door to my prison. *Honesty* was no longer a threat that hovered as an ominous boogie man threatening to convict me.

****

By the time I was a year into the program, I had a vague idea of how it worked. The twelve steps that I first saw posted on the wall at Chit-Chat and are referred to in the program as a design for living began to make sense. So, following the advice of my sponsor, I agreed to tackle them one step at a time.

The Twelve Steps of Alcoholics Anonymous

1. Admitted we were powerless over alcohol and that our lives had become unmanageable.
2. Came to believe that a Power greater than ourselves could restore us to sanity.
3. Made a decision to turn our wills and our lives over to the care of God *as we understood Him.*
4. Made a searching and moral inventory of ourselves.
5. Admitted to God, to ourselves and to another human being the exact nature of our wrongs.
6. Were entirely ready to have God remove all these defects of character.
7. Humbly asked Him to remove our shortcomings.
8. Made a list of all persons we had harmed and became willing to make amends to them all.
9. Made direct amends to such people wherever possible, except when to do so would injure them or others.
10. Continued to take personal inventory when we were wrong promptly admitted it.
11. Sought through prayer and meditation to improve our conscious with God *as we understood Him*, praying

only for knowledge of His will for us and the power to carry that out.

12. Having had a spiritual awakening as a result of these steps, we tried to carry this message to alcoholics and to practice these principles in all our affairs.

I'm not sure what my expectations were. Did I expect to be cleansed and emerge as clean as the pure-driven snow? Would I be struck by a bolt of lightning and have some kind of epiphany? My mind was wearing me out with all of the mental gymnastics, and we hadn't even begun.

For me, working the steps had become a **just do it** project. Left to my own devices, I would have over-analyzed it, decided I couldn't succeed, and thrown in the towel. That is why a sponsor was so important for my process.

I made it through steps one and two. I knew once I picked up that first drink I was no longer in charge of my actions or behavior. And in step two, I was willing to make the fellowship my Higher Power, understanding that the definition of insanity is doing the same thing over and over, and expecting different results.

When it came to turning my will and life over to a God of my understanding, I was a deer in the headlights. God and I weren't exactly on a first name basis. It wasn't His fault. I had come to the conclusion long ago that he was so busy with more important things, like taking care of others, that I didn't make the priority list. My job, the way I saw it, was to fend for myself. I didn't need any help.

In my early teens, I made a feeble attempt to introduce myself to God. My best friends were all Catholic, and I was intrigued by all of the rituals and mystery. So, I decided I would convert. I informed my parents that I wanted to go to the Catholic school, and they acquiesced. I sometimes wonder, if in my desire to want to fit in somewhere—

anywhere—I thought by donning the blue and white uniform of Catholicism that some kind of miracle would occur.

It didn't.

I continued to struggle with my lack of belief off and on for several years. Until it just got old and I no longer cared.

Every time I attended a meeting where God and the third step was the topic, it took everything I had not to bolt. I was beginning to think I would never get it.

Then one evening as I sat in a meeting I don't even remember what the topic was, I received my miracle. In my peripheral vision, a vague, ghostly outline of a white, pocked-marked door swinging halfway open appeared on the wall. I was standing inside the door, and an image of Christ was there on the other side, gently tapping. In that split second, I realized He had been there all along, waiting for an invitation to step inside.

Imagination? A hallucination? Who knows. It doesn't matter. It was the motivation I needed to move on, and I haven't questioned it to this day.

I would never have been able to progress to the fourth step, which is taking a personal inventory, without accepting the concept of some kind of higher power. The steps are arranged in a specific order for a purpose. The cleaning house steps which are four through ten all require at least a smidgeon of spirituality.

The biggest hurdle I faced in step four was coming to terms with how my disease had affected my children. Because I sought escape, rather than solutions, they had been denied a healthy loving environment in which to grow emotionally. Without realizing it, I had done the same thing I accused Steve of doing. I had taken my own children hostage.

Chaos and denial co-existed in our home. The only kind of attention that seemed to be forthcoming in our house was the wrong kind. I threw an invisible sheet over the elephant in the living room and walked around it daily, kids in tow. And every time that elephant began to disrobe, I took a drink. The atmosphere in our home was always charged, ready to go off at the drop of a hat. We were never sure what we did to trip the wire. It could range anywhere from me wanting money to buy the kids a birthday gift, or send them to a Catholic school, to Luke looking at Steve the wrong way. Nick and Jake learned to stay out of the way. They knew how to fade into the woodwork.

When he wasn't screaming and raging, Steve would sit in his chair for hours, exhaling vapors of stone cold silence into the mounting apprehension that filled the room. And if that weren't enough to intimidate us into supplication, he would fix his hateful gaze and stare into empty space for hours. The silence was the most frightening because we never knew when there might be a volcanic eruption. We could sense it, rumbling beneath the surface of our trepidation.

Family dinners were a treat. Steve was either raking me over the coals for something or hitting one of the kids over the head with a spoon. He rarely missed a chance to put Luke down. Whether it was in front of company or at family gatherings, he would repeatedly seize the opportunity to openly criticize him for the most minute transgressions. If it wasn't about something he did, it was how he didn't measure up to Steve's expectations. The look of embarrassment on Luke's expression mirrored that of whoever was being subjected to witnessing the ongoing assault. It was pure mortification.

Why didn't I defend my child? Because I was terrified, afraid that in doing so I would incur Steve's wrath even further and make it that much worse for Luke. So I leaned on alcohol, telling myself that the next day would be different. It would be better. A drink was the only thing that allowed me to live with myself.

By the time Luke was nine, he had already learned that he couldn't trust me. The incident that informed me of that fact is seared into my memory bank of failures. He had been invited to Mary's, his best friend's birthday party. The invitation appeared to have been an afterthought, arriving just one day before the party. Mary went to a different school so Luke did not know too many of the other kids. Wanting to make an impression, he decided to take his new phonograph and some records. Head held high and full of expectations, he marched down the front steps and across the street to Mary's house.

Twenty minutes later, I heard the front door slam shut. When I looked down the hall, I saw Luke, head hung low, dragging himself up the steps. The phonograph and records were left sprawled on the bottom landing. Before I could ask what happened, he brushed past me and went into his bedroom without saying a word.

When a child hurts, the mother's pain is almost symbiotic. The need to console him was an aching knot in my chest. I was determined to get to the bottom of whatever happened. I found him lying on his bed, staring at the constellations painted on his ceiling. As I lay down beside him, he turned away and curled up into a ball. When I wrapped my arms around him, he stiffened and moved away. The line in the sand had been drawn. But I refused to be rebuffed. The ache in my heart swelled as I stroked his head, trying to coax the pain from the wounded child that lay rigid beside me.

"Luke, honey. Please tell me what happened." The roughness of the worn chenille bedspread dug into my cheek. "Come on, baby." The lump in my throat was constricting my breathing. "You can tell me. Please don't hold it in." The dead silence that hung in the air thundered the unspoken accusation that prevented my nine-year-old son from confiding in me.

I don't trust you to protect me.

Hit with the realization that any further attempt to console him was futile, I raised my head, and left my failure drowning in the tears on his pillow; my tears.

Why was I unable to comfort my son? I had no excuse. It was the alcohol. It allowed me to overlook the mounting evidence of what living in such a dysfunctional environment was doing to my children and me. It helped me shove it down that dark bottomless pit where responsibility and accountability were buried, unable to surface.

Nick and Jake didn't spark Steve's animosity, he simply ignored them. That didn't ease the fact that because I was so adept at standing on my head trying to keep the peace, and escaping reality via alcohol, that they didn't also pay a hefty price for being raised in those conditions. They tucked their scars away in their invisibility.

Denial

A blanket of denial warmed me, tucked me in, and made me safe. I crawled into its cavity and curled up in the illusion, smothered myself in delusion. 'Tomorrow will be better,' it whispered. Take another drink. So I did. And for what seemed an eternity, nothing changed.

> weighted in alcohol,
> my caterpillar
> sprouted wings, but couldn't fly

Layer by layer, recovery skinned me like an onion. It spared no tears. It yanked away all of my excuses. Left me sprawled naked on the scorching beach of reality.

Answers preceded questions. Yes, I can quit anytime. The liquid courage, the coffin nails, the sugar-coated calories. What do they call it? Yeah, that's it. Comfort foods. Relationships...they belong in a category all of their own.

Okay, okay, I hear ya' Lord. Let's just do one at a time. We can start with the most harmful.

And we did. Thus began the wildest ride of my life. The uphill climb. Summit in sight...*Son of a bitch everything is real* equals S O B E R.

twenty-four hours
makes anything possible
one day at a time

The fourth, fifth and ninth steps were challenging because they required in order; total honesty, deflation of ego, and accountability. I couldn't have tackled them without Sara's help. She was the key to discovering the rewards waiting behind each curtain. She knew when I was ready to move on, explained how each step should be approached, and didn't allow me to beat myself to death in their execution.

One of the greatest miracles I experienced in doing the steps occurred one Saturday afternoon while I was agonizing over my failure as a parent. My pen refused to commit it to paper. In taking inventory, I had made a long list of my defects, offset by my assets. As suggested, I gave detailed examples of both. The list incorporated almost every area of my life, except for the most important—the one that caused me the most pain. If it continued to fester, I knew it could take me back out.

Crouched over the dining table, reading the same lines

over and over and lighting one cigarette off of another, I wasn't even aware that Luke had let himself in the front door and was towering over me.

"What are you doing there, Mom?" he asked.

Startled, I knocked the ashtray off the table and slammed the notebook shut. He stood there waiting for an answer. The game was up; I was never good at lying.

I turned around and looked up at the sober young man standing tall in front of me; clean shaven, eyes bright and focused, hands steady and no longer shaking. I was overwhelmed with both gratitude for the miracle of his sobriety, and shame for not having been there emotionally for all three of my children when they needed me.

I told him the truth. "I'm working on my fourth step."

"What?" Luke didn't bother to contain his surprise.

He pulled a chair up beside me and sat down. "You should have been done with that weeks ago. What's the holdup, Mom? Don't you think it's time to move on?"

Damn it. I could feel my lips trembling. I tried to hold back the tears. My kids didn't like to deal with a lot of emotion. It made them uncomfortable. Years of running from it, hiding behind false bravado, inappropriate humor, and in Luke's case, alcohol, influenced their approach to problems and solutions. To this day, all three prefer to deal on a cerebral rather than a feelings level.

When I told him I was stalled on the ugly reality of how much I had let he and his brothers down when they were growing up, he looked at me incredulously. The wisdom that followed released me from the bondage that was anchoring me to the past.

"Mom, *if* I can forgive you, and your higher power forgive you, then who are you not to forgive yourself?"

He said it so matter-of-factly that it began to make sense. He stood up, gave me a quick hug and was on his way.

64

Years of pent up guilt and shame escaped in a long sigh of relief. Luke had unknowingly given me the gift of freedom. I picked the pen back up, my hand involuntarily shot to the right-hand side of the paper under the column marked assets where I meticulously wrote the word *accountability.*

Once I was over that hurdle with less fear and trepidation, I struggled through the fifth step with my sponsor. Because we had established a relationship built on trust and respect, I was finally able to dump a lot of the garbage that kept me tethered to a past that needed to be released.

I was on my way…

Not knowing a lot about humility, my approach to the sixth and seventh steps was still laden with a bit of ego. Puffed up with this new surge of confidence and determination to get it perfect, I decided it would take me several weeks to uncover all my character defects, and at least, months to remove them.

During this self-imposed Odyssey, I could feel myself slipping backward. Recovery was depleting me. I was running on empty. When I realized that no matter how much concentrated effort I was putting forth, it was to no avail. I was like a dog chasing its tail. Running and running with no end in sight. Admitting defeat, I swallowed my pride and called Sara.

"I've been biding my time waiting for this call, Dallas." Her tone was conciliatory. "Have you finally worn yourself out?"

"How did you know?" I asked.

"Well, remembering my own struggles and misconceptions about these two steps, and knowing you; it was inevitable." She chuckled. "'I can do it, I alone can do it,' doesn't work here, honey."

There was a momentary pause.

"Dallas, go get your Big Book and open it up to the steps.

Read six and seven to me."

The term 'Big Book' viewed by many to be the Bible of Alcoholics Anonymous was so penned due to the thickness of the pages in the first edition and has no religious significance. It is, however, the basic text of how to recover from alcoholism. Its teachings, specifically the twelve steps, is used today to treat a variety of addictions. It was written by one of its founders, Bill Wilson, who was once thought to be an alcoholic of the hopeless variety. It has sold over 30 million copies. Within its over 400 pages, the personal experiences of many alcoholics are shared, along with a series of solutions, a guide to implementing the twelve steps, and much more.

I put Sara on hold, went into the bedroom and retrieved the Big Book from the bottom drawer of my nightstand. I kept it there to avoid any visitors' prying eyes and to protect my anonymity. Flipping through it as I made my way back into the living room, I wondered what it was I could have missed. "Okay, I found it."

"Now read it to me, just as it is written."

"Six. Were entirely ready to have God remove all these defects of character."

I still didn't get it. "Sara, I *am* ready."

I couldn't contain my frustration. "I've been working day and night to recognize and correct all of my faults."

Sara sighed. "Bet you are pretty damn tired after all of that work, aren't you? It's not your assignment, Dallas. Do you see that three letter word *God*? Quit trying to rob Him of his purpose, and allow *Him* to perform his job. And remember, you are not Him."

I looked down at the 7th step.

"Seven. Humbly asked Him to remove our shortcomings."

Suddenly the lightbulb went off. Sara remained silent.

"I can't believe I missed that," I said. "I read these two

steps dozens of times."

Sara's response was a real awakening. "Our egos tend to make us alcoholics feel that we are not only invincible but that we are all knowing and capable of superhuman powers. We believe we need no one. And when we finally are driven to our knees and admit that we can no longer do it alone, we understand what the word *humility* truly means. Now get on with It and humbly ask God to remove those shortcomings."

I did get on with it. I came to realize that I would always have shortcomings, and probably develop new ones in recovery. Each day I could humbly ask for them to be removed and proceed to do the footwork, which is my part. Understanding that the program is one of spiritual progress rather than spiritual perfection helped to minimize that egotistical, blown out of proportion, idea that I was somehow superhuman. Acknowledging my humanness opened up a whole new avenue of growth.

The fourth step became a template for completing not only the sixth and seventh steps, but it was a valuable tool in determining who I needed to make amends to in step nine.

Step nine must be approached with both caution and complete honesty. It reads: 'Made direct amends to such people wherever possible, except when to do so would injure them or others.'

I had heard of instances of those who thought they were in a confessional and spilled it all, not giving consideration to how it would affect others. In some cases, it did additional harm by not being decerning. Others, includes those who are making the amends. This step needs the guidance of a sponsor. It is not about getting forgiveness. It is about admitting accountability and apologizing for harms done. It matters not how it is received, only that it is offered.

I knew it would be a matter of timing. I prayed for the guidance to be shown when my children might be open to receiving the amends. Nick and Jason lived far away, so I decided to write letters to them. We rarely discussed my drinking. They didn't want to address it and preferred to remain in denial. They both imbibed, so any discussion regarding alcoholism wasn't a topic that came up on their menu. Feeling my way around our conversations, I was blessed with an instinct that led me to know when it was safe to make those amends.

The letters were sent about a year apart, and both were received graciously with identical responses. "Oh, Mom. You're not an alcoholic."

Remembering Luke's response to my fourth step, I decided to not rehash it with him. I was ready to move on. Or was I? Making an amend requires that it isn't wrapped up in a litany of justifications. Words like *because, but,* and *if you had* or *hadn't* need to be eliminated. There was one amend that remained, but I wasn't ready to do that yet. The apology for one particular issue that I owed my husband, now my ex, had to be shelved until I could do it without making excuses.

Twenty-two years passed. In between the fifth and sixth innings of my grandson's ballgame, the opportunity presented itself and "I'm sorry that…," spilled forth without any addendums.

Steps 10, 11, and 12 are ongoing. I try to incorporate them into my daily life. I continue to take a personal inventory, and when I am wrong, I promptly admit it. This still requires some effort and is rarely as prompt as suggested. But I get to work on that. I try to remember I am recovering, not recovered. And that it is a program of progress, not perfection. Seeking to improve my conscious contact with my higher power is approached through daily meditation readings, prayer, and fellowship with other alcoholics who guide and understand me.

And last but not least, the twelfth step, which I have found to be the most challenging: 'Having had a spiritual awakening as a result of these steps, we tried to carry this message to alcoholics and to practice these principles in all our affairs.'

I have no trouble carrying the message to those alcoholics who walk through the doors of AA needing help. I am able, without judgment, bias, or expectations, to reach out and provide a sympathetic ear and remain detached. But I find it much harder to achieve that necessary detachment when it comes to family.

Just because some of us made it into recovery doesn't mean that the genetic predisposition was left at the door. As time goes by, family members multiply, grow up, and in some cases choose to sip from the fountain of their inheritance. Remembering that it is not my job to speculate, preach, or round them all up and herd them into the light has been my greatest challenge. The fact that AA is a program of attraction rather than promotion was exactly why I didn't bolt, and why I am sober today. Those loved ones, who may or may not share my disease, deserve the same right to determine for themselves whether or not they are candidates for recovery.

Practicing these principals in all my affairs doesn't come naturally. Because these steps are in order, I can reflect back on each of the preceding steps and draw on them for support when I start floundering. I do this from time to time.

If I need to apologize, the 10th step lays it out for me. If I become self-centered and difficult to live with, I can go back to my fourth and sixth steps. If I become controlling and begin running on self-will, I need to resurrect the third step.

The AA program is a design for living. It is the tool shed I continue to go to, when life, with its many surprises, attempts to undress me and expose all of those alcohol (isms) that are never completely obliterated. Many of those tools are the same ones I picked up early on and continue to use. Meetings, sponsorship, fellowship, daily meditations and the steps, just to name a few. Recovery is a process, not an event. And everyone's path, though it may be different, requires the tutelage of those who have gone before.

Sponsorship

The recovery maze
requires deft navigation
don't *assume* you can go it alone,
if you think otherwise
pay attention to those
who still flounder about on their own.
Like it or not, we need someone to lean on
someone strong to shore up our foundation,
in the darkness, a lantern whose light is so bright
it won't matter how long the duration.

Committed to challenge our sponsors stand tall
never pausing—without hesitation,
they reach into their hearts, extend a firm hand
give us cause to expect a celebration.

So
to all you Lone Rangers, I offer this thought—
if you don't choose your Tonto
it may all be for naught.

****

Against all Odds

The statistics of those who make it into recovery and stay are as varied as the number of resources that can be found in studies devoted to the history of alcoholism and addiction. It is a proven fact that the odds are stacked against long-term abstinence. Yet when I totaled the number of years gifted my family, hope looms. One hundred and twenty-six years is a tribute to the recovery stretch that once seemed unfathomable. In addition to myself, my sister, brother-in-law, and son, my second son has put down the drink for two years and before my father passed, he donated five years to that total.

It hasn't always been a piece of cake. Learning to face life on life's terms without a crutch can be painful, confusing, and in some cases, seem damn near debilitating. In my search for sobriety, I discovered a plethora of other addictions was lurking in the shadows, waiting to pounce. And attack they did.

Shapeshifters

In the graveyard of my misery
Shape-shifters are shadow dancing
Addiction seeks another guise
To cultivate this soul's unrest.

Nicotine, food, and exercise taunted me. One year into recovery, I decided to quit smoking. Before I succeeded, I was chewing Nicorette and sneaking cigarettes. It didn't matter that the combination could cause serious heart problems. Every time I took a break from work, I would slip downstairs and have a rendezvous with the vending machine, stuff my pockets with Reese's cups, then smuggle them into the restroom where no one could witness their annihilation. I still wasn't convinced that I had an addictive personality until my sponsor noticed how it flexed its muscles at the gym.

Anger drove me to the gym. I was eight years into recovery and smarting from my second divorce. I didn't want to drink and knew I needed some kind of release. A rigorous exercise program would be just the ticket. I could kill two birds with one stone; vent all of that simmering anger that was about to erupt, and lose weight at the same time. I was so pumped up that I was making an intelligent choice that I couldn't see the warning signs cropping up along the way.

In the beginning, it was fine. I chose a simple routine, charted my progress and stuck to it for a couple of weeks. I wasn't dropping pounds fast enough so I began adding more machines and increasing my sets and reps.

As I worked my way up from burning two hundred calories a session to five hundred, I decided I could treat myself to a few (well, maybe more than a few) snacks. Everyone needs a reward, right? I became a slave to that chart; licking my lips and thinking about how I was going to spend that reservoir of vanishing calories as I documented my progress. By the time my sponsor burst my bubble with "Gee, that sounds just like addiction," I was up to four days a week, seven hundred calories a session and only three pounds slimmer. I finally saw the bigger picture. I could become addicted to damn near anything.

Addictive Personalities

Drugs and booze may be arrested
But that doesn't mean we won't be tested,
Addiction doesn't fade away
It hibernates until the day
It thinks we might be led astray.
A candy bar, just one, no more
Too soon turns into three or four.
We find we're just a drag away
From lighting up a pack a day.
The opportunities are endless
To enslave us one and all,
From relationships to exercise
Kching-kching casino's call.
Addiction never takes a break
Disguised inside denial,
A ghost that thrives inside its host
And threatens our survival.

Addiction is far-reaching. It contaminates every heart and soul it touches. It is devastating the very fabric of our society, as well as rupturing our values. It rips open the seams of trust and devours hope as it whips us into servitude. And if that isn't enough, it dominates the obituary columns with the unspoken stories of young people dying way before their God-granted time on this earth.

The alcoholic and addict are rarely able to define that point in time when the fun and socializing aspect of *using* becomes one of *need* and *slavery*. The progression of the disease, often unnoticed or denied, slithers like a poisonous snake down a dead end road, its sight always fixed on the final strike.

****

The good news, however, is that like all other journeys, there are safe detours around those dangerous areas under construction. There are a variety of paths offering hope: Signposts bearing the name Religion, Rehab, Therapy and AA and NA. Recovery is poised at each of these stations, eager to lift the burden of despair and to offer relief to every alcoholic and addict bearing its weight. Recovery is usually three-dimensional; choosing one path exclusively seldom does it. Sometimes, it requires the merging of several roads to lead us back into the light.

Crossing the Bridge

One by one, they circled the parameters of sobriety. Driven from their comfort zone by the scent of death and the gravity of isolation, the pack became fragmented. It was no longer cohesive. It couldn't protect them from the inevitable.

As they clambered across the bridge of uncertainty, the escapees paused and cast pleading glances across the abyss, encouraging the other members to join them. But it wasn't their time, the wounds weren't deep enough, the scars not yet committed to the annals of shame and regret.

> the force of the storm
> doesn't always rip away
> every leaf that clings.

Those who dare to take a leap into that scary, unknown territory called sobriety have a long, hard fight ahead. Every step forward is often followed by two steps back. People, places, and things have to be changed and new support systems erected in their place. Mental and physical cravings must be dealt with. Facing life on life's terms without a substance to rely on requires a commitment to self that goes beyond the norm. The process of getting sober can be a tug of war. But the rewards are so numerous and the joy so overwhelming, that a few rope burns are a small price to pay.

> a taste of spring
> followed by a harsh winter
> is my season of hope

The single most important thread that weaves its way through the fabric of recovery is the addict's desire to stop drinking or using. Not the desire of his parents; his significant other; his siblings; his children or his employer. Even though they may be the reason that sets him on the path, they must be left at the door. *Why?* Because many of those relationships may not endure the process. Seismic changes often take place in family dynamics.

For years, everything revolved around the disease. A survival template unknowingly evolved that allowed victims to cope. Maybe they got comfortable in their individual roles. Once the alcoholic or addict is sober, he may appear to be even harder to deal with. Perhaps, he is no longer apologetic and can no longer be controlled by guilt. Maybe he is so involved in his recovery and spending most of his time with people in his support group that loved ones feel abandoned.

Adapting to these changes isn't easy. Everyone has become ensnared in the grip of a disease that refuses to simply back off just because the alcoholic or addict is abstaining. Once it plants a foothold, it hangs on for life, trampling everyone in its wake. However, the same avenues of recovery are available to co-dependents. The same rule of thumb applies. To succeed, the focus must be concentrated on their own *recovery*, not the alcoholics or addicts.

****

It's damn near impossible to express all of the gratitude I have for the multitude of blessings that have been showered on our clan via the miracle of sobriety. My sister Gerri, who started it all, has been the benefactor of a twenty-year marriage most would kill for. She entered into it sober and brought to it all of the tools of recovery that enabled her to work through a variety of problems, including her husband's PTSD issues. Sobriety allowed her to confront and solve the kinds of difficulties that can gnaw their way through marriage vows. That union has served as a prime example of how it works for all of us.

I continue to remain in awe every time I think about my dad's courageous five-year excursion into recovery. How proud I was to be seated next to him at an AA meeting, knowing full well just how difficult it was for this strong, dignified man of seventy-eight to admit defeat in order to succeed.

The biggest miracle was Luke's transformation. At twenty-eight, the disease had beaten him to a pulp. Unable to draw a sober breath; deteriorating health; hallucinations and loss of hope, he was teetering on the brink of death when he finally surrendered. The road back was a steep climb. He grabbed his hiking boots and began the long, rugged ascent. With the support of my ex-brother-in-law, Jack, and sister Gerri, who already had three years in the program, and the love and support of our family, Luke walked through the doors of AA, determined to do whatever it took to take back his future.

Rhythms of Recovery

A tear pulsates to the surface
driven by the drumming
of
a recovering heart;
action marches
atop the grave of reactions—
buried in yesterday's orchestra pit,
while hope
dares to resin it's bow
on
the metronome of healing.
The vibration
of seismic change
rattles the cage of incarceration
and
hope emerges from the ashes.
Dressed in freedom,
it tap-dances across the stage
to the rhythm
of
sobriety's symphony.

When alcohol robs you of everything, reconstruction must begin from the ground up. The bricks and mortar that held Luke's new foundation together were named Jack and Coach, another recovering alcoholic. At Jack's insistence, Luke moved in with them and discovered a whacky oasis in the middle of a frightening world where everything he had done, and everyone he hung with, had to change.

Putting the gravity of the situation aside, the combined personalities of three recovering alcoholic bachelors, all of them control freaks, *sharing space*, made for one lively sitcom. It was Jack's house, and he was a meticulous housekeeper; Luke was O.C.D., and Coach was the original mold for Jerry VanDyke's role in the T.V. series Coach. The comedy of errors that ensued was the perfect distraction.

While Jack followed everyone around emptying single butt ashtrays, Luke kept track of exactly how many times a day he did it. Coach shouted out orders that fell on deaf ears. The Lord works in mysterious ways, but work He did.

In 1994, Luke went back to school and graduated Cum Laude with a double major; one in sociology and the other in criminal justice. In 1996, he took a job as a social worker in a mental health facility where he met and married the love of his life, Jana. Ten years into his recovery, Luke entered the field from a unique vantage point. He acquired his certification and became the lead drug and alcohol counselor at a correctional facility where he spent the next four years. Because he was able to bring his own experiences with him, no one could bull shit him. He had been down that dark, slippery road and made it back.

His most treasured experience occurred on September 26, 1998, when he and Jana gave birth to their only son, Dylan. Unlike his father's upbringing, Dylan has been the recipient of two loving, enlightened parents, who with the help of a huge, shared toolbox have created an environment that ensures safety and encourages self-esteem. My grandson has never had to experience the world of dysfunction wrapped up in addiction. Hopefully, he will be one of many missing links in our genetic cycle.

****

In 2013, the disease reared its ugly head again, compounding the loss of my mother. Jake came home from California for the funeral. Even though we kept in touch, I hadn't seen him for several years. I was so preoccupied with my own grief that I didn't notice the signs until the day he left. But Luke, Nick, and my nephew caught it immediately. The trips outside to the car, the smell of alcohol on his breath, and the lost look projected in his blank stare.

The day he was to leave for the airport, he walked to the bar around the corner, supposedly to say goodbye to a childhood friend who worked there. Luke was scheduled to pick him up in less than an hour. With the ticking of the clock, a familiar anxiety crawled its way up my reality. As the time drew closer, I decided to go after him.

Once inside, I was swallowed up by the dark, suffocating environment; a sharp contrast to the bright, sunny afternoon I left on the other side of the door. The long bar was nearly deserted, and I could barely make out the bartender in the dim lights. When I inquired, he nodded to a small room in the back.

For a split second, all the pain, the guilt, and the recriminations I had experienced during Luke's addiction came back to roost. It was as if a lightning bolt had catapulted me back to another dimension, and I stood frozen in time. It was surreal. There he sat, hunched over a shot and beer, staring across the room at nothing. I was so dumbfounded that I was unable to address it. We walked home in thundering silence.

The miracle is that Luke, who had twelve years under his belt managing three out-patient clinics at the time, *was aware*. In that hour ride to the airport, he was able to share his own experience, strength, and hope. Because Jake was already so beaten down and ready to admit he was an alcoholic, what he heard sunk in.

It has been three years since Jake tipped his last glass of alcohol. He is one of those few who has been able to manage without any outside help. He knows it is available and tells me if he needs it he knows where to go.

Nick, my youngest, has his own romance going on with alcohol. It doesn't seem to have beat him down *yet*. He has managed to acquire two masters degrees and a string of other degrees and certifications. He has a successful business and seems to be happy. Nick has always been an over-achiever and a workaholic, two slippery characteristics indigenous to the disease. I keep my fingers crossed and send up daily prayers. That is all I can do. He is aware of the family curse. Every now and again I remind him of that fact, in a subtle way, of course.

Most of my grandchildren are of legal age now. When I see them tipping the bottle on Facebook, I bite my tongue and cringe. We all had to learn our own lessons, in our own time. When I find myself wanting to overstep my bounds or am inclined to start preaching, I try to remember my own journey and realize that the last thing I want to do is alienate them. If they should ever approach me for help, I will share with them the Joys of sobriety.

The Joy of Being Sober

The joy of being sober
compared to being high,
is bound in every breath I take
in my desire to live—instead of die.

It's measured in the steps I climb
all twelve to be exact,
that stretch beyond burned bridges
and helps me keep my life intact.

It's sheltered in the smile I wear
In the fact I *can* care
In the love that I share.

It's tucked inside a template
designed to harness hope,
it over-rides the need for booze
or any other kind of dope.

The joy of being sober
compared
to being drunk or high,
Is the weightlessness that grew me wings
allowing me to fly.

Learning to live life on life's terms without a crutch isn't always a cake-walk. Life continues to happen whether we are present for it or not. Sobriety allows us to have input. It gives us a choice on how we respond to both the good and the bad. Instead of following the pack into oblivion, we discover we can take another path. The choice is ours. It always has been.

Sobriety
fires the kiln that allows us
to mold our own clay.

Epilogue

Next month, I will be giving a lead (telling my story) at the Women In Recovery's annual luncheon in my hometown. Instead of employing charts and graphs to help illustrate my journey, I will get down on my hands and knees and gently slide out from under my bed a torn, faded, twenty-eight-year-old collage that was my introduction to Therapy 101 and share it. Little did I realize at the time, that the tear-stained barrage of pain, confusion, and smidgeon of hope, would be my portal to recovery.

I was stumped. The assignment was to create a collage that reflected my feelings. *What feelings?* I was a flat-liner. It would take a backhoe to dig them up, that is, assuming I had any.

I gathered up an impressive variety of periodicals; Psychology Today, National Geographic, Time, and an armload of artist magazines which proved to be invaluable. I grabbed a pair of scissors, a bottle of cheap glue, and spread the large white poster board out on my dining room table, all the while mumbling obscenities. I stared at the sterile blank space demanding to be filled and wondered why I was so frustrated. How difficult could it be? I'd just shuffle through a handful of pages, slap them on the stupid poster board and be done in a couple of hours.

Wrong. The project became an emotional roller coaster that took days to piece together. A churning storm of suppressed feelings began to fight their way to the surface, becoming a push/pull exercise of endurance. Bold, glossy metaphors depicting feelings of isolation, rage, emptiness, confusion, and vulnerability populated about eighty percent of that damn poster-board.

I set it aside and left it in plain view for a couple of days, taking stock of it each time I passed it by. Every time I looked at it, it became a little less volatile. Then, when I realized what I was feeling was relief, I intuitively knew it wasn't finished. It needed to reflect that glimmer of hope always there but rarely acknowledged.

I scavenged through a huge bin of old greeting cards, some dating back to when my kids were toddlers. I shuffled through years of happy calendar events; Christmas, Easter, and birthdays of all my family members. I pulled out a birthday card that I had sent to my grandson when he was five years old but got returned for insufficient postage. When I showed it to him on one of his visits, we both had a good laugh. I plucked it out of the bin and immediately affixed it to the collage.

As I did so, I knew at that moment, the grandkids translated to my harbinger of joy. I went back to one of the artist magazines and cut out a beautiful gold orb that became my sun and placed it directly above the card.

Joy composed only about ten percent of that depressing portrayal of how I felt, and what I thought about my life up to that point. But it was enough. That shimmering, sliver of hope clinging to the edge of that poster-board became embedded in my DNA.

Over the years, a metamorphosis occurred. As I worked the program, became less self-absorbed, and began to participate in my own life, the fear and anger receded into the background. Little by little, the ugliness lost its grip on me.

Today, if I were to stretch that collage around the room, it would be populated with a majority of positivity and an attitude of gratitude. Even though the pain was real and lurks in the rearview mirror, periodic upsets now and again can trigger it. So, I continue to remain vigilant and rely on the basic principals of the AA program to get me through the hiccups.

****

Alcohol is an Indian Giver. Everything I thought it gave me in the beginning, it snatched away in the end. Instead of being witty, I became an annoying bore. That self-confidence and self-esteem I craved became self-loathing. I was about as courageous as the sniveling lion in *The Wizard of Oz*.

And last but not least, that avenue of escape that I had relied on for so long became the dead end that gobbled me up and spat me out.

But all of the above and more has been restored to its

natural state via recovery. As long as I don't pick up that first drink, hopefully, I can remain an example and extend my reach to those family members who may end up on the other side of that bridge, baying at our family tree.

About the Author

Dallas H was born, raised, and continues to live, in a small, friendly city in Northern West Virginia. In addition to being a recovering alcoholic, she is a proud mother, grandmother, and great-grandmother. She is also a part-time employee at a local bank, a loving sister, a loyal friend, and a poet. Dallas considers herself to be just another run of the mill alcoholic and refuses to allow that aspect of her makeup to define her.

In 2017, Dallas will celebrate 30 years of continuous sobriety. Although she understands that that fact will not negate the genetic pre-disposition that curses her family, she hopes it may have a positive impact on those grandchildren and great-grandchildren who may be at risk.

It was important to her to share her story in order to help others. This is Dallas H's first book. To contact Dallas, please visit www.writtendreams.com.

CPSIA information can be obtained
at www.ICGtesting.com
Printed in the USA
LVOW10s0447170517
534668LV00001B/64/P